BLACK SALT

Poems by Édouard Glissant

Translated by Betsy Wing

Ann Arbor

THE UNIVERSITY OF MICHIGAN PRESS

Translation of this volume was made possible
by a grant from the National Endowment for the Humanities
under its Fellowship Program for College Teachers
and Independent Scholars.

English translation copyright © by the University of Michigan 1998
Originally published in French as *Le sel noir, Le sang rivé, Boises*
© by Editions Gallimard, Paris, 1983.

All rights reserved
Published in the United States of America by
The University of Michigan Press
Manufactured in the United States of America
♾ Printed on acid-free paper

2001   2000   1999   1998   4   3   2   1

No part of this publication may be reproduced,
stored in a retrieval system, or transmitted in any form
or by any means, electronic, mechanical, or otherwise,
without the written permission of the publisher.

*A CIP catalog record for this book is available
from the British Library.*

Library of Congress Cataloging-in-Publication Data

Glissant, Edouard, 1928–
   [Sel noir. English]
   Black salt : poems / Edouard Glissant ; translated by Betsy Wing.
     p.   cm.
   Includes bibliographical references.
   Contents: Riveted blood — Black salt — Yokes.
   ISBN 0-472-09666-4 (cloth : alk. paper). — ISBN 0-472-06666-8 (pbk. : alk. paper)
   I. Wing, Betsy.   II. Title.
PQ3949.2.G53S4513   1999
841'.914—dc21   98-44381
                                                                             CIP

Contents

Introduction 1

Riveted Blood
One Single Season 19
Lava 29
Mirrors 39
Seasons 45
Frosts 53

Black Salt
The First Day 63
Carthage 71
Salt Taxes 79
Africa 85
Wounds 91
Highest Noon 99
Acclamation 107

Yokes
Yesteryear 115
What Begins 121
Wood of the Heights 129
Malemort 139
Monomagic 145
Whatever Opens Up 151

Introduction
by Betsy Wing

*J'écris enfin près de la Mer, dans ma maison brûlante,
sur le sable volcanique.* —SOLEIL DE LA CONSCIENCE
[*At last I write close by the Sea, in my blazing house,
on volcanic sands.*]

Black Salt brings together three books of poetry by Édouard Glissant written during the period 1947–79. It was first published as a single volume by Gallimard in Collection "Poésie," a famous paperback series devoted to the most significant work of the major French-language poets, particularly those of modern times (such as Ponge, Char, Michaux, Rimbaud, and Mallarmé). Although Glissant wrote and published other poetry during this period, the *Black Salt* grouping remains most clearly representative of his poetic project and its evolution, representing important moments in Glissant's trajectory as a writer.

Glissant works, and reworks, in many fields at once so he is almost always engaged in writing simultaneously a novel, philosophical/political essays, and poetry. The subject matter of one emerges with different modulations in another and later will reemerge in other texts, not quite repeated. Glissant's own description of this practice, with its inherent notion of the fragility, the erasability of words and their enduring power, is "a spiral retelling." All of his writing is undertaken as a process of knowledge, where the knowledge—always possible and always incomplete—would be a "thorough, thick (opaque) experience of the world (*Poetics,* 12). Though best known to English readers for his essays, particularly *Caribbean Discourse,* and the one novel that has been translated, *The Ripening (La lézarde),* over the years Glissant has consistently turned to poetry as the ultimate striving for knowledge of the totality of the world. For him the poem is the form most suited to this *totalité-monde,* which can never have one meaning or one conclusion but is the precarious synthesis (as is the modern poem) of more and more distinct realities. Beyond this, for Glissant, "Language," as Foucault has said, "is no longer linked to the knowing of things, but to human freedom"; Glissant sees in poetry—the language that brings what is potential into reality—a means of locating the multiple possibilities for a new and productive relation with the world.

Glissant's view of the power of poetry coincides in some measure with the Surrealists, particularly as the first great Martinican poet, Aimé Césaire, understood them and their relation to modernity. It was Césaire, with his shockingly avant-garde introduction of post-Parnassian writers, such as Lautréamont, Rimbaud, and Mallarmé into the conservative curriculum of the Lycée Schoelcher, attended by Glissant in Fort-de-France from 1939 to 1946, who introduced the younger generation of Martinicans to the poetry of modernity. Césaire's analysis in "Poetry and Cognition" (1944) of the modernist movement claims for himself and André Breton (also in Martinique, along with numerous other French intellectuals, during World War II) the heritage of Rimbaud's "lettre du voyant"—its "incredible seismic tremor." Césaire went on to reject a good deal of his irrationalist, surrealist connection, particularly insofar as it related to political issues. By the 1950s, as James Arnold suggests, real change began to take place in the relations between European culture and the former colonies, and Césaire, while remaining a writer of major importance, moved further into the pragmatics of the political. But his early insights into the power of language to transform the world touched the young Glissant profoundly: "Poets have always known. All the legends of antiquity attest to it. But in modern times it is only in the nineteenth century, as the Apollinian era draws to a close, that poets dared to claim they knew."[1]

Glissant, too, has been politically active, having sufficiently angered the de Gaulle government in 1961 with his organized opposition to the creation of the départements d'outre-mer (DOM, French overseas departments: Martinique, Guadeloupe, and Guyane) to have been arrested, denied access to Martinique and Guadeloupe, and placed under surveillance. While the Antillean situation has changed over the years, however, Glissant's geopolitical work has remained constant in its passionate attention to language. His writing is a continual search for the language, an Antillean French, that, no longer constrained by European standardization, will stand on its own and will make both himself and his country—the plural Antilles—heard in the world. Through moments of optimism and hours of pessimism Glissant continues to believe that only human imagination is capable of all things, including changing the world.

The earliest poems here, those of *Riveted Blood* (1947–54), begin to lay out the project. Their inscription "for every tortured geography" takes us directly into the struggle of the alienated poet (in self-exile to higher education in France) to write and be written by his island land. *Riveted Blood* celebrates not only the countries rising from the ravages of colonialism but also all geography—all writing-of-the-earth. While frequently personal in tone, the poems insistently cross conventional borders between personal, emotional contact and contact with the world-totality the poet is struggling to know and put into words. This poses several problems for translation. On the most basic level there is the question of raw material available in each language. Always the forms of intimate address (*tu, toi*), whether the poet is speaking to himself or to someone to whom he is close, fall by

---

1. Aimé Césaire, "Poésie et Connaissance," in Lilyan Kesteloot and Barthélemy Kotchy, *Aimé Césaire, l'homme et l'oeuvre* (Paris: Présence Africaine, 1973), 114. Translated by James Arnold in *Modernism and Negritude* (Cambridge: Harvard University Press, 1981), 58.

the wayside in translation, though the effect may occasionally be given in tone. In addition, French is able to leave the borders between *he/it* (both represented by *il/il* or *le/le*) and *she/it* (*elle/elle* or *la/la*) undefined. It is left to the reader to decide if the subject or object is a person addressed, a state of being (beauty, solitude, etc.), or a preceding element of the concrete world. This ambiguity was particularly vexing in the final group, "Saisons," in which each poem is, indeed, addressed to a person and in which the title in four of the five poems is a noun ("Glory," "Beauty," "Solitude," "Temptations") that, in former poetic eras, would easily lend itself to such personification. In general, though not invariably, the best solution seemed to be the use of the pronouns *he* and *she*. The feminine element, in particular, needs to be stressed in English, to retain the easy gender connection it has in French with night, the sea, and the land (*la nuit, la mer, la terre*).

Glissant's attention to the harsh or succulent details of concrete existence saves the text from anthropomorphic/anthropocentric excesses despite this sort of personification, now more pronounced in its new English version. In French, while harking back to the expansive rhetorical gestures of a poet such as Hugo, this border crossing would also be an example of Glissant's already developing vision of the world as being composed of entities on equal footing one with the other, whose mutual access has become a contemporary reality. On another level person, history, and land are explicitly merged in the poem entitled "Elements," and "Avowal," a poem that promises to be so purely personal, soon moves into history. Glissant's words "I am in history to my barest marrow" apply.

In translation the surface play in the "original language," particularly when homonyms are used to lead the reader to unexpected places, is hard to reproduce where it occurs, and Glissant makes some use of this technique. His poetry, however, does not depend on it for its strongest effects, which lie more in accumulating rhythms and images. My practice here has been to drop the wordplay in one place and resurrect it elsewhere. For instance, in "Avowal" the word for "winnower," *vanneur,* stands where context would have made a reader expect (retrospectively) *vannier,* "basket-maker" (26). In "Solitude" it was possible to reenact this poetic process: in a poem full of sea images the "night rises up white corral" (*toril blanc*) where less complex expectations could be satisfied with "white coral" (33).

More important, the title of this first group of poems, *Riveted Blood,* contains wordplay that cannot be brought into English without introducing an overintellectualized technique such as double titles separated by a colon. This would be totally foreign to Glissant's practice. But something interesting has been lost: though *sang rivé* is primarily blood that is frozen, fixed, glued, rooted, pinned, it could also be blood characterized by shores (*rives*). The poet, undermining our expectations for the relationship between the words *blood* and *riveted* (being riveted by blood, at the sight of blood, would be more usual) forces us to set aside such expectations about his particular relationship with the world—his difference. Then, in the poems themselves he makes this difference clear in his own terms, inscribing this point where blood is riveted as a moment of a very particular alienation—an instance of intensely experienced suspension, isolated and fixed between two magnetic fields, between the shores of Martinique and Europe, both truly in his blood.

Glissant's poetics in these early poems is strongly marked by several principles defined in part by their relation to their opposites, which he eschews. Setting himself apart from the followers of the Symbolists, he never attempts to write the unsayable, the inexpressible. The premise of his writing is that all can be said. His would be a poetry of duration (*durée*) and accumulation, as opposed to the poetry of the revelatory instant, the momentary fulguration epitomized for Glissant in the work of Rimbaud. Glissant does not seek privileged moments of individual revelation that may come from some external source or even from "deep within." He strives, rather, to locate himself precisely by the concrete contacts produced by all his intelligence, sensory as well as intellectual, in touch with the world. The words of these poems are part of the physical continuum of his existence—frail and receptive, powerful and resistant, dense and alive: "I say that poetry is flesh" (15).

This poetics came together during the early years in Paris, when Glissant was involved with the avant-garde literary scene as well as with the proponents of negritude. His particular development, however, while constantly in contact with these elements, began to be more deeply influenced by writers who might seem to hold little appeal for a poet from one of the now former colonies: St. John Perse, Paul Claudel, and Victor Ségalen. Certainly, Perse was not given good press by Glissant's old guide, Césaire, who furiously parodied Perse's scenes of an idyllic Antillean childhood in *Cahier d'un retour au pays natal*. But Glissant read Perse, as well as Ségalen and Claudel, as poets whose quest to know the world and come in contact with the other left traces to be followed in his own search—much later to be formulated as a Poetics of Relation.

The writing techniques of all three of these poets reflected their desire to open the formal enclosures of French culture to the outside—the world beyond. The abandonment of established French metrics, an enclosure whose parameters were set by the alexandrine, went hand-in-hand with their interest in experiential time, the time of *durée* (duration), as Bergson called it. The poetic line could be formed on the basis of human breath rather than syllabic counts and stresses. Claudel's first *versets*— as these more open poetic shapes were called—did not stray far from earlier metrics, often being composed of several alexandrines arranged in the form of a *verset,* and his thought inevitably returned to the universalizing concepts of Christianity. Ségalen and Perse, however, reinvented the form to suit the voices they were seeking, with Perse even pushing the alexandrine to speak in "prose." The incantatory attention to details of the world accumulating in a sweeping time full of histories but incapable of measurement by dates fits this form and fits Glissant's purposes.

This poses, then, another problem for the American translator. Our most open, contemporary verse, in which Whitman stands as the great liberator from imposed formal constraints, took as its rhythmic basis not the first levels of human breath but, rather, human speech—and not at the level of oratory but at the level of idiom. So the grand gestures to which French poetry has always been accustomed, and whose scale became even more expansive in the imaginative order of Perse's *Anabase,* have almost disappeared from our poets' repertory. This is, of course, an oversimplification of American-English poetic possibilities; Whitman, certainly had an ear for oratory. Still, there are few highly regarded English-speaking poets in our day who "write poetry in what is called prose,"—as T. S. Eliot, justifying his reference to "this poem [*Anabasis*] as a poem," described it. There are fewer still who would take the *Song of Songs* for their verse model, and this is surely something one must hear behind Perse and now Glissant and something I have tried to convey when it is present.

St. John Perse (1887–1975), whose influence on Glissant has frequently been remarked, has been known to English readers for many years. Glissant's formation, however, is equally marked by Victor Ségalen (1878–1919), whose works have only begun to be available to us in translation in this decade. Only three of Ségalen's works were published during his lifetime: *Les Immémoriaux* (1907), *Stèles* (1912), and *Peintures* (1916). All are products of his refusal merely to integrate bits of foreign, "exotic" decor into a European vision of the world. His unfinished work *Essai sur l'exotisme,* redefining the notion of the exotic, was not even published in French until 1955—that is, during the period in which Glissant was composing *Riveted Blood.* Defining and fixing the "sensation of Exoticism," Ségalen describes it as "none other than the notion of the different; the perception of Diversity; the knowledge that something is not oneself . . . the power of exoticism is simply the power of conceiving other."[2] Furthermore, his project is not to describe the Exotic but, rather, "rigorously avoiding whatever is banal about it (coconut trees and camels). Move to its wonderful savor. Not try to describe it, but point it out to those able to be exhilarated by its taste."[3]

The sensuality of perception is never lacking in Ségalen or in Perse. It is for both poets the first level of contact with the world that provides real knowledge and is not to be overridden by generalizing concepts. And for Ségalen it is the guarantor of the dense reality of self and other: "Exoticism is not, therefore . . . the perfect comprehension of something outside oneself that one would embrace within oneself, but the sharp and immediate perception of something eternally incomprehensible."[4] Glissant will later develop this concept of opacity, claiming specificity as the right of every people—the right of self-definition in relation to the other—the right not to be reduced according to some universal model. For Ségalen the poet in contact with this incomprehensible difference will be able to convey it. The hieratic, compressed forms of *Stèles,* in which the foreignness of things presented seems to have been turned and examined and polished and worked thoroughly in words, stand as powerful examples of his aesthetics of diversity. Things must stand alone, stunning to us in their sharp separation, but it is the poet who can show us where to look.

Over the years Glissant has honed this aspect of his work, until, finally, in *Yokes* (1979) there is no need for the translator to worry about the porous borders we saw in *Riveted Blood.* The practice of merging man and the world, individual experience and histories, shifts into another part of Glissant's writing—the essays, with their composite voice of merging genres and converging histories, and the novels "of the involvement of the I

---

2. Victor Ségalen, *Essai sur l'exotisme: une esthétique du divers* (Paris: Fata Morgana, 1978), 36. Translation mine.
3. *Essai,* 36.
4. *Essai,* 38.

and the We, the I and the Other, the We and the We"[5]—leaving the density of concrete existence as the subject and object of poetry. The poems of *Yokes,* unfortunately, do not stand alone as well in English, in which they tend to be more elliptical than concrete, and I have provided some notes to contextualize specific elements of the poet's vision, thus violating my intent to follow Glissant's poetic practice as closely as possible. In these poems Glissant only points once, but, on the assumption that relation is more important in this instance than detour, I have pointed a second time at things without echo in a non-Martinican experience.

None of this information concerning influences, of course, is essential to the understanding of Glissant's work. For purposes of translation, however (and concurrently for a reader who might want to understand the successes and failures of this translation), it has been useful as an aid to developing an American voice, one with an inner consistency that is responsive, that relates to outside contacts. Particularly, it has provided some hints of which direction to take when faced with the inevitable compromises of translation.

The central group of poems here, *Black Salt,* provides the title for the collection. In 1960, when it was written, the pressures of the negritude movement were strong, but Glissant, ever unwilling to be defined by institutionalizing forms, pushes beyond the Africanizing tendencies of "black writing" of the period. In these poems salt—found throughout the earth, part of the bodily composition of all life forms, and generative of certain moments of human history—is the important element. *Black* is its adjective, and it connotes the darkness of the depths of the sea, where salt is formed, or the earth, where it lies hidden in vast accumulations where the sea has been. It is primarily the

---

5. Édouard Glissant, *Discours antillais,* 153. This passage is rather differently translated in *Caribbean Discourse,* by Michael Dash; however, the almost impossible polyphony that Glissant risks in his novels seems to me better demonstrated in my almost literal translation.

color of "the salt of the earth"—all that is basic to life; secondarily, its connection with Africa is inescapable, but for Glissant this connection is in the dark strata of forgotten memories rather than some sacred, totalizing root.

The seven cantos of *Black Salt* sing of the past, present, and future in a continuous, unbroken voice, moving through tones of lamentation, demand, and acclamation and forms that are occasionally as different as plainsong and formal verse. Their flowing voice in French, beautiful when read aloud, makes up for their ellipses, so that the accumulating rhythmed images build their own poetic logic. Césaire's "Poetic Propositions" are pertinent to the translation here: "The music of poetry could never be exterior. The only *acceptable* music comes from beyond sound. To go in search of music is the crime against music that can only be the beating of mind's wave against the rock of the world."[6] When something has had to give in compromise, it has seemed better to maintain the sense of breath and beat to convey Glissant's music than to attempt to reproduce the fluidity of the French language.

"The First Day" deals with the salt of memory and birth, in which the first taste of salt came with mother's milk and lingers only in the imagination. In adulthood the poet, the reflective self who speaks and is spoken by the words, now confronts the sea, knowing he is both formed by it and contributing to it. The poem is full of the vocabulary of the sea, some of which is common enough Martinican French. For example, *héler,* "to hail" means simply "to cry out" in Martinique. Names of winds, boat parts, ropes, sailing techniques, all turn up in these poems, as part of Glissant's drive to particularize experience.

The pretexts for these cantos are occasions when salt has intervened as a determining factor in history. There is the salt of the sea of the Middle Passage as well as the salt rubbed into the wounds of slaves. In "Carthage," in which the Punic Wars deter-

---

6. Aimé Césaire, in Bernardette Cailler, *Proposition Poétique. Une lecture de l'oeuvre d'Aimé Césaire* (Sherbrooke, Quebec: Naaman, 1976).

mined that Rome would rule the Western world, rather than sharing this world with Africa, the Romans pillaged this great city and laid waste to the surroundings by scattering salt on the fields to render them infertile. "Salt Taxes" refers to the cruel imposition of heavy taxes on European peasantry who later would become equally cruel and oppressive slave traders and colonizers. In "Africa" salt is the substance over which powerful tribes went to war against each other.

Beyond these pretexts, of course, the salt and the sea exist on a symbolic level: the salt of human suffering produced by the dark sea that covers not just the deaths occurring during the Middle Passage but, by extension, all oppression, with its vast and complicitous silence. Structurally, the cantos are held together by the speaker, the *conteur,* the *mesuré diseur,* of the poem, who both reflects upon and is within the trajectory of *Black Salt.* Sometimes lamenting, sometimes ironic, sometimes joyful, and sometimes solemn, the poet opens an Antillean vision of time and space for us to hear.

The final group of poems, *Yokes,* presents language problematics that are starkly different from what we have seen in *Riveted Blood* or *Black Salt.* Published fourteen years after his return to Martinique, they have none of the expansive lyricism that embodied Glissant's hopes for his country but reflect, instead, his attempts to grapple with the spiritual aridity produced by Martinique's increasingly pathological dependency on France. The poems, in comparison with the earlier ones, are almost saltlike, dry and crystalline bits left by a formerly lush existence. "We have eaten the forest," Glissant has said, describing simultaneously the measures taken by a starving populace during the World War II blockade of Martinique and the careless consumption of the land's beauty. The compression of the poems, however, though turning its back on the lyrical voice, owes less to a Mallarméan drive toward silence than, once more, to Glissant's concern with the concrete, which in these poems becomes intensely visual. They almost bristle with particularity, outdoing

Ségalen's *Stèles* in their startling opacity. This opacity, however, is an essential component in the one hope Glissant does see for the Antilles. By remaining in place, the people of the Antilles can "renaturalize themselves." The poetics of this space/time is yet to be constructed and, to be durable, must be built of materials as hard to work as the rock that is the source of the storyteller's cry. "He is grounded in the depths of the land; therein lies his power. Not an enclosed truth, not momentary succor. But the communal path through which the wind can be released."[7] A steadfast persistence in conceiving and speaking, without apology, one's own reality is the first step into the world.

Glissant's words—our epigraph—"At last I write close by the sea, in my blazing house, on volcanic sands," come from his earliest published work, *Soleil de la conscience* (Sun of consciousness [1956]). It is but one translation. "Enfin j'écris près de la Mer" can be also translated "Finally I write close by the Sea," that is, "in the end this is how I always write, the place from which I write." Of course, it is both, but for me it is in *Boises* that the breakthrough occurs, where, finally and at last, Glissant has written to "revive, black in the rock."

Here is Glissant on translation:

> Translation is like an art of running away, that is, in no uncertain terms, a renunciation that fulfills.
>
> There is renunciation when the poem, translated into another language, has let escape a very large part of its rhythm, its secret structure, its assonances and those random chances that are both the accident and the permanence of writing.
>
> This escape and renunciation must be consented to. This renunciation is that part of oneself that one abandons in every poetic practice to the other.

---

7. Édouard Glissant, *Caribbean Discourse*, translated by Michael Dash (Charlottesville: University Press of Virginia, 1989), 237.

What the art of translation thus teaches us is thinking that is sidestepping and skirting, or the thinking of the trace, which, contrary to system's ways of thinking, shows us the uncertain and the threatened, but something uncertain and something threatened that converge and strengthen us. Yes, translation, art of the light touch and art of approach, is a practice of the trace.[8]

Though fugitive and ephemeral, as every translation must be, and conscious of its losses, this version of *Black Salt* only asks to open a trace onto other words.

Acknowledgments

In addition to acknowledging with gratitude the support of the National Endowment for the Arts—in the days when such was possible!—I wish to thank Édouard Glissant for the patient hours he devoted to reviewing these translations with me and the willingness with which he occasionally changed a line of the French so that his poetry could more easily enter the American language.

---

8. Édouard Glissant, "Le Cri du monde," *Le Monde*, 5 November 1993, 28.

Riveted Blood
(1947–54)

for every tortured geography

No work pulled tight, silent, and monotonous as endlessly sculpted sea—but outbursts concessions to earth's effervescence—opening past worry and torment a stridency of beaches for the heart—bursts always dislocated, always reiterated, and beyond consummation—not works but the matter itself where a work makes its way—all bound up in some project about to cast them away—first cries, naive murmurs, weary forms—witnesses, though awkward, of this project—which, as their imperfections meet perfectly cohere—here with the power to convince that we must stop at the uncertain—things that tremble, waver, and ceaselessly become—like a land in the grip of devastation—sparse.

One Single Season

Eyes Voice

Torches loomed in the black color pond of the night
Our soluble hands our look of plunder like timber the lit straw
    of our eyes!
Seas, across you my silence patiently rekindles
Across you are rims across you mud
And the conjunction of freeze and thaw.

Of old of old
Ah! rebel, stony memory in the canebrake.
Every bush of memory hides a ready shot.

Upon our heads the beating of the mill
Fierce fires crackle in our nights
No matter what you do the cry takes root.

November

And the oar is earthen expecting a new land Oceania love of you is a bandanna topping a mast Oceania love of you a coconut-palm of fog in your presence Oceania in the shadow of your cathedral shrine to savagery and I am taming the foam of your robes Asia and Europe in our childhoods Asia is a coral dwelling within itself and gnawing at itself between skies and battle and as for Europe it is a field of nails. No longer to hear the red stirring of wild butterflies and a heavy day. More and more fierce the elections of murderers in the lovely cancerous rain. Oh the loveliest where our skins are crammed in the loveliest oh in the desert cowbell fingers of lianas from the bush, Africa. The final mission was to lead the word astray into teeming deafness scorched Tropics. Like an addition of fruits drunk with memories in the banana-trees' mute desire.

Wild Reading

From the hill direction a whole expanse suddenly shoves its
  cart into dizzying splendor
In the factories' mill my poverty smiles over powers of the
  earth
In the cane scars in shins forever black
The water so often called for reddens to my caressing voice
Rebel now from irascible depths of embrace my leap into the
  standstill.

Like the hougans leafed out in patience
ah the sole evidence I desire is the last voyage of my lassitude
  among the dry leaves of a monsoon
the flowering of islands the frothy geography of islands on
  eviscerated seas
our hymns our brows barred from sources our feet crammed
  with storms

Cut cut with your long stroke of dawn where birds try in vain
  to nest
Between the tom-tom's links in spite of me the earth capsizes

From the wind direction like a gash shoulders thrusting into
  the sparks
Nights of impressment all night.

Rock

Foam rain head heralded water's beatings rain

oh my faces' deliverance the light-like embrace the gnarled
    joining of these two rivers the preview of the storm
I roll callous the water the wave the foam I bathe a rock I
    a rock the sea lazes in my gulfs the sea floods my presence
foams the landscape veers a convergence sprouts the line of
    the horizon goes by at the primal scene of my joy the trees
    dedicate to me the dry flight of their leaves
the mud of gullies flows toward my purity its patient
    rumination a quay
slowly rots away its silty peace

And my senses remerged my skin granular I exhale
my house my solitude Taoulo my voice
whips pounds Taoulo hisses

and from the irascible heart of its womb the earth whips up
    dizzying splendors
the rain beribboned air bears down upon me o straitjacket air

Taoulo hails and near me time lays down scarves of yellow

and time snaps up the invisible speed
rotting idleness of wild mango on the rock.

Slow Train

Words I have fed with fire laid with the flesh of men and the
   lianas of scrub forest
scrub brush that grows in flesh exposed to the sun of clearings
   now
I have opened the blazing pod of a louvre lying in wait for
   frozen orangutan eyes of mine

It is land when peacocks between boas and giant brambles dare
   no longer fan
by dint of thinking land I explode land is when you gather up
   brains splattered in the trash bin of the new ocean
rivers imagine games where my veins are a hopscotch of
   freshwater for the spring to run dry
I feel myself a child in the trough of terrestrial sound doomed
   to plunderings and solitudes
the sea carves out a friendship where I lay my joy down, word
reviling the snow of streets as slave ships' armor
They provided us amphorae in the frigid heart of this last day
   we have slept in torrents and moons slept in the skies
They have cut us back driving tetanus into the scrubgrowth of
   pores
Of course the canals were dry and the auvergne beard of rain
   merged with despair
shiver house brine of rough diamond
fish in the cage
asleep

The Tree Great Tree

Your branches the stench of desires of blind haying of arms of
   the sea
Your leaves a wound from the Middle Ages within the memory
   of my splendors
your branches the shoulders of a furrowed woman left thirsting
   with sharp grasses
tree your body renewed I peeled from your body this carapace
   of my lights
your trunk of replenished inner leaves
your trunk of light in the black night-blooming field
your trunk of root that took trunk and wondrous thing bed of
   the trundling snail
your sprout your roots the frozen fire of your roots and the
   masses of men who clutch the dugs of your pain

suffering like winter struck into deepest wellspring

Black Smoke

Mad mad eyes without bread, blooming the blackbird's cry
   from elderberry shadows
(it is the fourth star on the left if you go along the master's
   glance)
like an enameled street engraved into the breathtaking torrent
   of totems.

Lava

Elements

Suns extinguished among hairs of the real sun! I shall regain a health of fruits ablaze.

Here are the knotty notices, on the trees, fed with leaves. Animals are friends of mine in flesh. Rivers flow through me toward the transparence of lands here I am
In this forever dew young girls weave on their faces to proclaim love In this hubbub buccaneers loom into clearings In this burgeoning of suns dispersed by sprinkler trees I am the one who is river impassive rock and the ardor of the land within its breast
We are thunderbolt the hand caressing lightning the hand proffering I have held between my fingers the shaggy coat of night I no longer sleep spearheads by my head I no longer live on the cayes next to caimans washing in cool water I scrutinize the sand and the sky is up against me, with its glaucous eyes Shadows are hostile toward me Nothing less than a splendor the melting down of waters and the barren bray of seaweed.

You, who struck up hullabaloo and giddy fever of the forests. With sheer gulps in your forest of stars you erect the nights' funeral pyre In your forest organs (my unknown life) the day's fires of salvo. With full gulps, the suddenly risen impending land, beyond the poem's breathable waters, you play sun, you are winning. To sleep in the river to dig in the silence Leave your hands in the scrub of the Atlantic Between mornes suddenly burst open by July O freedom of tears in the land among reconciled trees And through the safety catch of suspended logic.

It is a country flogging haunches against blindness Races races arrows of assagai cane I snow and freeze beneath the baobab's tambourin
What others write
In capital stars
I feel it ruminating gently its flowering spread its multitudinous compasses between my arms. Birds arrow to the crushed thirst of the volcanos. Whoever would sew silence with a white thread has no right to the drunken tourney. I say that poetry is flesh.

Also, grinding with its sole tooth (of storm of blood of tear) great lick acceptance. One jaw of sands deserts and scrub, that the other be of stars and pollens: may he hurl into it the stars the broken necks the whip the master who sepulchers and canes that hiss waiting and pain and blood, his poetry and his noisy blaze of poetry. Like, interweaving unheard-of tropic levels, the dark gap in the wind. Listen,
leaning upon silence
trumpetings.
A dew of galleys fallen in sea salt meadows A flash in the sap I have decanted green water red water, reaped murderers cane and gourds Drink up The sun is a lantern sighted and shot down Splendors, travelers of the foam!
My house woven in defiance of lightning bolts, from rushes that eluded hougan's October blaze, my house my sea crystal house long wall of America. The rebel blacklisted for teaching children that there is only one finger to a hand. I brew the

bracken of waves. My waking is a dog's dragging his kennel under bridges.

Errantry caught in a trap, outmoded
when when and when the fleshless
bells of the inaudible?

I am in history to my barest marrow. Secularly ensconced: in this midday I spoke loudly as ignorance: it rolls its gravel inside me. I am waiting, gnawing of the poem, roses Yes

I am fragmentation
in nocturnal
music.

Man coolie-sailor sea-foam Ah the dew of my hair that you took for an eruption of snot coral Not a voice but a murmur Drilled built Blacks

Not killed incinerated decapitated but lynched I move along in coal strata My power layered onto powers! Clowns, now on their feet. A fine fuss. Here in the name of poetic plagiarism, to testify to moral splendor. I force myself to salute: man, this luminous desire for song. Vocative, much too.

The forest suddenly shouts toward life. Stars, prowlers, swarm into the locks. Alive o alive, queen. Your feet take the path, forsaken mango trees. Your skin inside out is a red furrow. Alive,

oh alive my morning of meadow you my night of meadow desecrated by bullfights. Into the water you slipped the gasps of your silhouette cut from glass. At the ford the black beach the black sand of caresses. In the star lovely star of your hands. Peaceful slaughter of dawns in the burned out hull of your dreams, and your voice shouted glory, of chaff mixed with chaff: I suspend the storm upon your lips' altar of repose.

Ah suddenly
the fear of being two
within beauty.

The lightning of you tresses of snow the lightning of you air and love interwoven. You snake and lacerated. I foam of your footstep.

And so I was, colony of martyr children of found dogs of unconverted dogfish. Oh suffering, rattling of wind in the streets. Poverty is ignorance of the earth, what is imagined is passion.

But no spluttering, no sun, now that man's open mouth is all that waits. Let us move on to other continents.

Rock resonated
Man plundered alive, furrow
Storm stained oh
for you I am blood, wondrous chalice. Roots, roots, I shall never be done with tugging on your prolific dugs

this wave I thought final now chosen by the fire to encompass me.

The Nourishing Air

In the trap of horizon the talon to untangle childhood mysterious
my white cruelty inebriates man the one I occupy the one offering me his slow flooding face the one who allots me his cities or simply his agony all make me more beautiful than tears' appearance in the valley more beautiful than the tearful valley between three blasts of the death conch I am inside the tower of silence like a white bird

From seas to seas through nitrogen sweetness leads back to the water's door beautiful visitor
Froth of rains delicate aggregation of dewfalls
I alone volcanos drain toward me their breasts bleeding open why
except that I arrive within myself air made fruitful with air of torture of oblique continuation

and I crawl in a returning round of dawns of middays more distant my brothers dead in exchange for dead stars (tatters of our flesh in space) you male female and permeable and similar and dissimilar

You seas so many attempted shipwrecks in your hands you men you snakes you towns walk in the gut of the earth do not crisscross me with beacons I erupt worlds worlds

The void is steaming bowl one predatory morning
The thieving void oh to live at its throat

Flight of sparrows in the sardonic river
At my shoulders at my flanks a day
Will stop earth turning within the prison it tells me.

And try, captain, as you will gymnastics of your red irons on
    my lips shall never drive me to this bread marked with the
    stamp of my discounted flesh,
Rain keeps you among the islands, Atlantic probing slavers, so
    many storms defied to save us that speck of your boats'
    putrid air.
The secret-keeping rain odors me with song imperceptible on
    my back ferns of rain on my hands knotty sheets of rain
    onto the welts the burnt feet the too conspiring sea

Through tunnels lit by sap and the eye keeps searching
    through starry streets whose sap roots are burned
I wait for rain velvet drill of pond waters beneath the waters,
    bursting its light against the nostrils of mules, their ears
    pricked for it rain and sun together

The only body mine now is free for rains of underground
    encounter oh rain from craters blazed with verdure
Ploughing its worlds among me.

Mimosas have closed sensing sparrow wings the pulp of rivers
Pedant for a change I reconcile insistent suns the whiteness of
    streets
O singers stuck in air's onslaughts, you, stars thrown to the
    singers

I hear through the mountain whose caves perceive (nostrils and
 ears) I hear metallic fragrance solemn mendicancies
The blindman eats his bread, the tree rests upon his double

Because beautiful the poem imposed on the late hour
 ploughshares of heatstroke where necks lay fallow
The manchineel's billion stars milk boiling in the cool of eyes.

Mirrors

Cities

On the wool of sound some object of silence one so immense.
The issue is love, its turning toward solicitous shop windows.
Who stops who gazes? Here thought arranges the display of
   rags, and charm lingers on and on.
There, giant cats scratch the earth, the steel of silence and faith
   with no object.

The Avowal

Each face is an appeal broken mirror
Weighing in their hands the despair
They face, trembling they are silent.

It is how they flower, avowal.

Space leaving those hands
No trace of friendship,
Secret so secret.
Who dares say if his face
Attaches to his body or if its surface
Is transparent?

Mirror, impassable, oh cliff.

She is bird pure impulse
Consumed by wind

Have they piled their loves
Soul on soul the way we see
Your marl your peat your chalk
O laborers waylaid by wind

Apothecary of terror
In his shell-field lit
The spark, dead women's ring
For a forgotten dead man

See, the poor winnower
He wove the willow of caresses
You the recumbent will have no peace
Until it tarnishes the mirror.

O the road scatters the man who tortures
He shouts abuse, contaminates
Offends and sets himself above himself
To attack in an absolute of silence.

Solitude moves him dies
He draws near the sea, mutters
Remains defeated, shattered avowal.

Cold Weather Fever

Ashes canebrakes oh your days
By eternity are forsaken
And like fancy dress your lies
Are tears mirrored into life

Shallow mirror and high tower
Death-water no ocean can confine
Beyond the digging hoe the plow
The fever and the furrowed clay

Weep that my space may bind
Space more complete upon you
Than any ocean makes an exile

My fevers furrow canebrake dead
And ash again for all such lies
More than eternity are clay.

Seasons

Glory

for Jacques Charpier

Unbridled queens of the new azure rise from their country.
River of leafage, and path of morning,
Of dawn itself, of blue skies, and the horses whinnied,
I saw you glorified and saddened by the old words,
And this mirage this sunset flare,
Mares now so familiar, and tamed.

And like a druid in supernatural forests of the past, you gathered
A midday. There time and the future married, and you welcomed their wedding.

Flames. Stampedes at midday's gate. May this whole song
Of muds and rivers descending the day's aplomb
Provide you a place of order, of thirst, not of carousing nor sudden blindness
And may you not be lured to harvest mistletoe of other times.

To Die, Not to Die

for Jean Laude

Fragrances dried on the beaches of my stars. Foam from the heights has no dazzle, the book is there, and its reaping.

Book of paths scant of water, book of the Dead book of Lethes, in this Northern land occupied with crops, beneath oh underneath the earth.

Open, in the Book nights are splendid. (The sea measured its fruits and its salt. The summer of night lit the summer.)

I learn I learn there is a battle, love never will return, is dead; and the field lies empty, there no combatant fought, field of the lone and eternal defeat.

And see the water meant to bathe the dead; the wife has spread it where the clergy step.

Death and its ferrymen are abjured
For leaving the vast sea beginning in a heart.

Temptations

for Paul Mayer

Lassos you leave us in the white day whiter than summer snow
Blind ones you rope salt to countless loosened storms on your
   bodies traveled by dreams of days now gone

When we love words catch fire and tear you roam about
For you love infringes upon heaven and you have only deepness
And you have only caves and cliffs for your desperate bodies

When we plow you stay you are snow beneath the crust
What do you say asleep under thick layers and in the fiber
You who disturb and enthrall us so?

Are you mere ghosts where impure wakes reside
Or roping just yourselves, lassos to bruise and tempt us?

Solitude

for Roger Giroux

Mast snow has lashed down with silence
At the suddenly saltless beach
He knows the sea he breaks the shore's face
And escapes the wind where moons fall in love.

Night comes she comes she rises up white corral
On the breast stirred by a wind of prophecies
She hollows no vessel of frenzies or livid love
But an absence of light.

Oh perfection of the undone oh law of the morning
The wind the solitary joined restores
In this chalice of body a sweetness
To him like a son to caress.

Daughters of sea! Men of salt! Gods smiling on the revels!
Oh nuptials unending.

Beauty

for Max Clarac-Sérou

It is here somewhere a wind of solemn roses it is blue sky
Weaving into foliage, unreal and such lovely hands
It is summer stripped of its dream by the wind, the naked
   child
Weeping in the face of day, awaiting noon.

Your city comprehends you. Scarcely a word begs this invisible
Breeze compelling us to boast of transparencies
A breeze in its sap more secret and unspeakable. See
Salt masks the season, the russet trees, the child.

We name the impure incense of unreal roses.

Frosts

Abrupt

No song, array on your desert
But innocence fallen red
Alluvia of the dead strata in your death
A cry letting a dead man silt up his wound
A cry a knot a plumb and heavy drop of heads
No song
But this stone in your hand where wind cries
And wounded birds fruits and words dream on
While quick you take by surprise
Blood riveted alive in a night with no sea wind.

Stay

Sampan in the horizon lay too many paths and a jungle lay beneath the mirror a thousand black chalks a wound lay how many tears a bay

Sampan at night down your paths the tears and chalks came back to us in the horizon lay just one mirror for this wound and beneath the jungle our bay

Sampan dreaming (dying born) we hailed you our forest the eagle cross and for our dreams your span and on our lips your vow

Here is the stay leading now from us to us giving the year where all appears (like a smile that lies in wait for us to catch us already mid our bornings).

The Dead and Living Tree

One whole night on the rim of the horizon
He sought you, not daring to shout over the gold
Whether you were crying among dead birds
Or giving voice to populations
Or coming silent woman through the density of windows.

He stood close to the night among the trees
He arose in its dawn and dead
He loved so dearly from shadow he hauled this sound
And set you, you pure in whose hands grew
Midnight flows of lava pondered within the tree.

He stood before the night
Held up by glacial wind
And eagles with no city rose

A dole of beggars bathing the horizon.

Black Salt
(1960)

to the sea

For the salt it means.
Brilliance and bitterness once again.
Lights in distress on its expanse. Profusion. The theme, knotted with foam and brine, is pure idea. Monotony: a tireless murmur cracked by a cry.
There—on the delta—is a river where the word piles up—the poem—and where salt is purified.

The First Day

The storyteller weighs his words unmeasured in the bright burst. He will sing, in his very solitude, of the earth, those who endure it. He offers what he says not to those it delights, whom it elates; but to bodies burned by time: thickets, peoples under duress, naked villages, the crowd on the shore.

Then, as this wise sailor, this measured speaker is finished by his song it begins him again. He enters, mere child, the first morning. He sees originary foam, the first salt sweat. History, waiting.

I

Mud runs down from the mornes to redden cane-knives. Presence, o great waters! A man in what he says regulates the haze of flaming torches, he sees

The image raised by his breast, his words. He knots night, canes and waters together. He tells of clay on a body, and then this word.

He cries out.

I was in this lament, listening to the night.

II

Old days. Nubile days. Shot through with spaces. Masts!
The first salt kept in the cup of a weary hand
O light, morning to reset you on your time.

A huntsman cries out in surprise, he leaves,
His skin tasting of dream and bitterness,
Dawn wavers, ah how beautiful to sink down again
Through the sea of silence, this fluency where you sparkle,
Dawns! As for myself,
I regret nothing. Time is there.
Other stars will sing
In this towpath of ravenous dark.

III

Men will come down the road of mud, they will come in, so arduously will they expose their bodies to the slow task. Afternoon wind covers the rooftops. The women raise a pure flash in their eyes, the dogs head down for the sea (to find bright banquets of dung and vermin).

Look, the sea has sent me off toward fertile day, O from so far off I head out with the waves still toward this absence and this face.

And if this taste of tangling lands is all you retain of what I say, I have not wasted my time nor vainly squandered the straw of this heart.

IV

The poet-priest recites his knowledge to the bright trees.

And they tell him: this word not from you holds you in its grip, dig for your words. —He says:
All my phrasing is in this shoreless river, where mudflows rise. They rise, silts cover us. Who speaks to us of digging?

On the thick waters I heard this word. I was the sprout far from gold treasures, I was pollen and wind. The sea collected the clay and the whole island keeled over.

The poet-priest recites his learning, and the earth actually veers, and leaves can be seen from below, vigorous and dark.

V

Untie your soul, arise, and contemplate this land. Walled in
Death keeps us apart, and your eyes have set the seal on
    mourning.
We can only enter through your gaze, but it is closed. For us
Your face alone will share the nuptials. Only your face.

Who are you? The horizon scarce contains you. The plain
You see loosened here in this dawn O pure indeed
With its frame of mud cries out to us of death.
Who are we, in this clay run through with blood?

The song purges you, you falter. Only your memory grows.

VI

Untie your soul, earth, moored to your cry.
Close, eternal, see. I see winter growing here,
And middlemost aloft your heart. The old flash

Matures. Old love subsides.
Open in succor to us your dying roads.
You were salt in that snow and that snow was only night.

VII

Realm whose cry is marble and fire blaze.
Silos, that night-long tempted me—I have seen night.

Be bright and brim, and with one hand the man sweating over
    canes can give you a place of rage and friendship.

He has cut already six times twenty bales for the woman who
    bales. —O grant, I answer,
I be as murky as this night predating time
Murky things suit us madmen who handle and untangle
Worlds, chaos, swords knotted in the naked sky. —And I
    answer:
Winter that plucks me from your skies, I have seen
How rare this passion and how deep, this sea.

VIII

Obscure designs hatched among the branches.
They were birds, wings and sounds barely astart
With murmurs, but the shoreline hummed and open skies
Surrendered to emotion's rise. It was dawn.
And the sword. The wake. A bright village hoisting
Its roofs and straw bedding toward the sky.

All that I cry is in the trace where salt has been.

IX

Farther and farther strives this word at every dawn
Toward thickets, climbing vines and sand. Toward the sea.

Lovely gentle people, so stubborn and serene,
I hear peoples, O splendor, I hear.

Name them. Hail them. Time is there. Summer
Has spread on the snow like black absence. The day
Finally, with these words, is set ablaze.

X

Deeps O tides.
Birds, dying at our sides, with sound of bygone days
Villages, weary rivers, so many fruits, so many swords.

You become a mirror for this face, sea glory,
Like a cold downpour between life and us
And the saddened maddened wind O wind.

You become a face where the mirror fades and you
More ardent than our voices in this track of time
Become voices of the hunter hearing you.

XI

You, salt of the realm of my hands now. I, like someone
Dumbfounded, plunging into the sea, who sees die around him
The night with its shores, what torches
Tell, like rippled shoals and great waters keeping quiet.

And reviving in the first morning. He knows
Sparkling night, blazing fires, the sole fruit.

XII

Like someone among bright trees being born in the rigging.
This is the final night. Tomorrow, stone by stone
Will be chosen. And like a sculptor of bones from blue sulfur,
He sings the bitter night open to salt and a woman
Sadder than the sun's nubile body at the blaze
When the sun's fire, dying in itself, is altered
Within the day and its blaze.

Carthage

Salt already on gravediggers' hands. The dregs of the sea, no longer aroma, is spread on the conquered city. Everyone forgets the first salt he tasted: now traffics in its essence. The world—and more countless the pillaged Carthages today—feeds this burning fire within him to conquer, to kill. The docile sea is his accomplice.

A people comes; to be allotted its share of salt on digging wounds. Finally free it bemoans the ashes. Salt is forever mixed with the blood of victims and with the wounded stones that were men's work.

I

All round the globe soldiers have built cities ruthlessly lousy with girls, who, girls and cities, lay down in this muck. Beaked galleys plow the sea, clamorous in fear against their prows: the dogs are coming! And men come behind them, legions.

Get up. Watch out. City, you burn already. See.
Dogs, men, beauties, your heart so soon destroyed.

II

Glory was in this heart, rims, black sand
In this heart silence: torments ravings stupid gnawing.
There the morning sweats yesterday's blood from rock.
In this heart is the heart of massive granite blocks, a word. The
    woman
Dropping in his hands her veil of dress
Suddenly leaves the bright streak of road, gives herself
Not to hear the city, at the foot of the rocks, imploring.

III

She goes by the sea, and praying by the roots,
Flees far from this word and falls on the sand.
She falls. Unknown beauty from the sea, the wreck
And present of a deeply sordid wedding in our midst ah
Water purifies you, you are ravished by its foam. Night

Abruptly descends upon you. Here is the spear, the woman
   tracked, the blood.
Conquerors, a woman at your feet pleading for mercy.

IV

Could you tell of this city, the storm surrounding it
And walk among the rocks off Numidia
Of this door slowly closed and the old men
Nailed to the wall by drunken soldiers and the man,
Impassive, on the tower, deflecting from his soul
The long wail of children hurled into the sea?

I have seen the cold sea that rolls in, waits subsides
Takes into its flesh the old healing dittany, the young flesh
As an offering, something due it, or a sacrifice on the high
   wind
More immensely calm and receptive, more unchanging
Than the November sky where vultures court.

V

The sea cries but its cry soon evaporates. And the soldier
Swells it with corpses, itching prurigos. The sea
Willingly takes its toll, its prize, is leased
Put in debt to life ebbing its dizzied array
Onto the shores, in tolls of dying song. A word
Awaits you, sea, you've not yet drained the cup, a word belays
   you,
Sea. And a hundred towering rages will turn the blue of
   charnel
Before your ponderous turmoil brings forth the gold
To make the High Season of the City dazzle.

VI

Between my life and me stands this ghost of my life
Dead disowned an awkward love submerged
Get up, night has stormed the city
I hold out a silent watch in the tower under siege
I see legions oh solitude harrier hawks
The slave's throat slit the master puts on his blood for cover
No joke: dogs! One blood good as another.
Bitter smoke cloaks the red morning, the dense dark.

Bodies debased, iron muzzles, this fire's froth
Guts strung out right to the inferno, the woman
Has fled the sea to share the flames, is here now
Wide open, arms spread to the horizon. Between my life

And me a black span opens, I reach out my hands, I cry
Into the fire endlessly rekindling.

VII

The towers collapsed, gold sloughed away, the lords as well
But there were slaves, a whole slew who went off
Oh conniving night toward the south, the forest, oh night

And manhandlers loudly mark humans down
They pile up jewels, wash this blood off pearls
They tally hard dry figures, argue, dogs bark
(Toss them a bit, that they blindly tear apart!)

The sea wind sultry sea wind covers the city its blue air
Fingers rotting bodies, frantic, the violated wind
Like a woman reaches for the horizon.

VIII

Grasses weep no longer beneath the wind. Neither the seaweed
Nor the Sacred Altars standing in the ashes nor
The Port where hawkers are on the lookout, stirs. (And the
    Altar
Spelled it out: I am the inferno's flame. —The Port
Opened every morning to wares from the Orient.)

Hear beneath the silence, city, a wave a cry
Fade not quite away then rise again, you shiver
The sap opens a bay a wind a lily into you
Midday carves things dry and eternal on the heights.

IX

Salt! Oh Salt and whiteness, heart of famine, impure digging
Naked shadow that the woman fled so long! Word of the sea,

Clamor! And thorn without the moldy earth, dreadful agony,
    pale sheet
Of noontime, oh wound. And the Roman, out of boredom:
Here there'll be a lake and a mirror, he says. Here
Parched seagulls that always fly by will come. —You, sea
This is the last shout of your revels. In this eternity,
You come to love the heavy silence you were.

X

Inside your glacial self you roar your solitude. And man
Made immensity his slave, the sea his fruit.
Your strength is there at his call, in hostage hands,
Is scattered by the hostage on walls, on the earth and on
The bleached eyes of a corpse slowly rolled back over.

Have you come to die in this ruin or to see for yourself
How a place grew rich on salt? Have you come to see
The extent of this blood brought down your paths: whiteness
Where sometimes nothing grows but shoots of drunken light.
    And I
Shall clear your eyes of their taste for safe darkness, that finally
You bemoan this blood, this place, this death.

XI

As salt is cried for the vanished woman, a livid
Scipio cries for and derides your soul. Will you let
This sorry creature contemplate the deserts you created, saying:
How peaceful to rest here on my bed of fears—
Then he tastes the salt, imagining the Games he'll give.

Still will you let your vast vertiginous cry
Die at the feet of a man who thirsts for other blood? You
Will you give your body, this fire in your guts
Still, and the path of your sterility, to someone
Who glories in or wearies of such sport?
The sea, now silent, runs away. Leaving me its foam.

XII

The men, the lancers, leave. And the dogs. O city
Silence and death now render you so pure. The slave
Leans toward this cry from your shroud, he says at last
The sea is calling! And in one's hand its foam
Is like a rock where wind puts many dawns, a black salt.

The sea beneath the galleys is at work. A standing cry. The
    woman
Hauled against the wind hurls abuse and bites and laughs at
    last.

Salt Taxes

Thatched hut. Straw and mud. In the distance the king's cavalry. The father wants to save his dilapidated house, but how? They will burn his feet, hang him from a tree to make him talk. The woman puts away her treasures: cauldrons, bowls, hoes. A boy pokes among the sticks, he will bury this bag now in the meadow. The Dragoons will sack and burn. The donkey will die, the mother weep, the eldest son be taken away.

So, cry for the glebe. See it by a sea it has never known. Let another come from farther still and teach. When granted, time makes for wisdom and salt for flavor.

I

    I have seen you glean your bodies, you were skeletons, Dead Men with barren scythes conveying only the harvest of your bones. When you hid the dour treasure of your stubbled hut, praying the scent would rise to heaven, away from human nostrils, I was where your effort ended. I saw your bodies, lowly fruits, and the Dragoons fed upon them. I have known you as the incense of their carousal; you were the roads they walked on! O to your own death scorching death pursues you. Gruel is your lot. A lacerated voice your lay. People of the land of France that levied you in the sweaty damp of fall: to die there among falcons and thorns.

II

I waited for you, serfs, beside the seas. Here the eager
Surface. Then rocks. The swaying foam.
Like traces on the sea of a massive flight of sora.
Night died in day, wrong died in summer.
Thus cruel death thus smells of drought
Died, to make acquaintance on the sea.
And you, living in a bright death.

—Who, the one hailing? What sea flows overhead?
And calls us to bathe the tower in oakwood fire?

I am the lowly witness, the command. You are hands
Bitter hands singing in bitter whirlpools.

And you,

    In this bright burst and amazement you are
    Mute silence emptiness the storm
    Where the black hush gripping me cries out.

III

Night is barely molting, it half-ends, suddenly descends
On humus: the part of me that strains, chafes, and cries.
Time stirs gentle wings, linen of dreams
Spread it over the sea, to quiet and to hide.
Time cries: You are but furies at the approach to shore.
Ravening questions, hungers, tracks of raving birds.

IV

And reply. From us flees the sea, the horde of shipshrouds gone,
Towards a sun beloved, a July and children.

Seashores cry music for men of fleeting soul
Who take the sea in their hands and consent. It flees.
Now the foam of song is fragile, and man consents.

You are the hands being bled for wild extravagance
Crafty peasants trod by horses, and lovers mad to pull apart their chains
Women open at the king's cry
Salt receivers yet having neither salt nor swill. I see
Other nuzzles, hands dead without a sound. I cry out. Beauty upon you!
You who know salt is sudden and black.

V

Just as the salt in day's fortress escapes
And as the salt dries in a hand where sea
Left the foam of her breast
As no one ever will exhaust the night, no one from this hand
Will drink of love,

Thus vainly have I levied firewood from your ash
Kept your barns, your crops, the storehouse you closed
And dawn was empty, still more dry the rose.

VI

The only sound is blood convoyed here by sea. The only storm
    one of blood
The acrid odor comes upon us, breathe it in, my swells. The
    only sound
Is that dim incense of peoples caught by the fire of our time
Who die bearing the deep of seas and the reek
Of most high and distant planets.

VII

Thus near the rocks once hurled at heaven, that fell
Like sad games of a titan or foam tossed by this love
I see the air throb with burns, I see thatching
The cool earth where the salt was put, the waves' stable
For a horse they carved up, that whinnies in the flames
For a heart ripped to shreds now sinking softly in the sand
Like savage toys of a hurricane, swallowed up.

VIII

Beauty upon you, serfs. You within this book—under kings,
priests, under captains, mirror-silver of this praise-song and its
   blood—where you wander, saying
Who will turn our wounds into knowledge? Who, our hungers
   into fees? Who haul up the silvering for us?
(Still saying: O! May the wind not go dead.)

And I shall name you Serfs and Martyrs, fires, vow
Deeply black. And different gods and highest up.

IX

Grooms ridiculed before their wedding, where the wife sat
   down to banquet, History
Who let down her hair, gave birth to pigs,

This word I cry, desert where you wander, jungle
Striped by your nephews' sword, doing what they did to you.
   Where is the salt

That made you suffer so and with such passion?

X

   They go, sometimes hailing, sometimes gathering that sea-dust. There's no salt, no storehouse now, no barn; and dried the rose. I stand, hailing this remainder of the day. By your side, serfs, one not of your blood, burning the tide as he goes. Against the city he sees the woman, the beams there like her hellish hair. She is the Legions' victim, rose of the sea. And huntress near the tides, in search of neither salt nor firewood. She held out her hand, where suddenly the sea glistened, so much have we cried. There, this forbidden Salt, that even from this distance we spy borne off to morning shores.

Africa

I saw the distant land, my light. But she belongs only to those who make her fruitful; within me, not I in her.

The tribes waged war for the custody of salt; nations raise armies to learn to savor. May the tillers of night also drink at this morning's spring. —Another land calls me.

It is Africa, and it is not. For me it was a silent land. Listen. Everyone is dancing, in the just ways of his body and his voice, in honor of the eternal fire.

Oho o tumblehaired one you spatter here
Finally I know the weary child who wails inside you
I recognized the man providing you with sea
Beside him robed in sea steps the woman of Africa
Whoever dares name her, she answers, he sees his queen.

Oho Maidservant so long turned into exile
Into magnificent desire, yet desire both absence and vow
As if in a dream where there was a queen but no royalty
Now weeps the man asleep, at his feet the sun of day's close
Entwines death and the tree, naked with no fruit or altar of
    repose.

And you o faraway unbeautiful one kept watch
But your piercing beauty burgeoned worse than screams
    beneath the skin
Made great beautiful howls of all that brooding your beauty
Flowed formless into floods and innocent went off to chase the
    clouds
You the darkness the fury you subsidence so slowly

Vaunting the fragrance or the act, measuring ire
Or phrasing the bright blast of your heights is not my aim
Nor meddling with the sultry parade of perfume you become
This is not the sentence branded by your forests on my body
Not your salt in my eyes unless it is salt I dreamed

Oho nameless Mother of these works named
By my heart, you secret heart of this voice, listen I cry

Not seeing if it is nighttime for the sun, not debating
If the word now has been cleared of torture, see
Now I have left behind me splendor rites and fire

And they told me: Harken, this song is no poetry
But parable, thing of surroundings. —Did they count
The stanzas before us sung by death? Did they
Those landless lords, see the pulse in this fire's face?
They told me it's a lie, but to them the sad world lies

Going and gathering this river where you silted down to me
A river you are since I began collecting rivers
Like a bouquet of throbbing flames, like sundered tears
In a bunch never dried by impatience
There I saw the huge quake and swell of your cry

Far ahead of us I saw the dawn you became. The night
Watched over the world in dull, dense herds, then the wind
Enmeshed our eyes. Mother, we grew for you. And when
Night embroils its nakedness with wind, should we
Then sculpt flowers, polish clouds, howl as dogs bay

And all this noise of the world awaking, wild
After a long massacre and longer sleep, the fire
Fierce in love with your dawns, the sky cast
From crime to crime toward your unreal heights, child
Sky, huge body that the star will unbridle

Oho mother o regent in your secret blaze
So long dreamed of so long concealed
You open now the tree where sleep desires
The queen rises within you, here, in your cry I leave
And like seaweed bind my clamor to your root

You are dark weather and dazzled light oho
You make me thirsty for you whom I never tasted, you were
Distant thus and clouded with words, this lookout

Inside me, who signaled, cried famine to laudless days
Called to the humus and to the dogs drunk from sleeping on it

I hear the year pound its toneless cry on your trails
I hear the land's slow drum of stumps torn out hear
The land in a mouth and a vigilant word
Like the drumming of tribes ready again for war; all
Salt heat on the pagan hands of enemies. Feel

Bitter need twist your body to no avail, famine
Where winds javelins seas and rages, surprised forests
The wind's mesh licks the firepot clean, children cry
A hut burns, a warrior dies, pastures smoke
Famine in the burned-up sky, and famine, in your vigor

And in the monotonous sealed word I hear famine
Oho words of our bloods here now hammering out the time
Of days flung fourteen times into the dreadful fire
I see this heart braided with fire, frizzled days, the blood
And in the loot this pinch of salt tasting of burnt grass

The ones who came to salt like dogs to quarry
You had no sky night kindling nor spear
Even night left you, even night, you burned
Forests suns and winds on your javelin spike
They freighted the flesh of your naked sons

The sky dammed you up so long in snags
Salting down this body drunk by dumbfounded years
Water source scuttering through the devastation you cried
Uprooted life, you cried, starless sky
And we at sea, fouled cadasters, knotted islands tied

For this transparent salt allotted you by Paladins
Knights of blood beneath their wine-pitted shields
For this loot you gleaned on the field of history

When they reaped the harvest of their ignoble glory oho
So many fires lepers so much night, and no pardon

O you are Voice and their arrogance will run dry. Lost
They are before the bare light and red like the bays, wind
Of seas hurtled against coral and abysses
Where more than one people has dug into beauty into heights
Lost lost voiceless victims nights shivering desires

Oho disentangler it is time to card this time, to weigh
With sea for scales and for measure the black salt
Sown by the blood of peoples who died, all
The only mother for you is the beauty hauled out
From torrid seas and blue chill of springtime Hear

Great ship! You who tangled nights together and loftily name
   us
Time in all flesh, cuttings in every spear grown
Whole lands have flowed from this voice, it is poetry
And a road to us was put up from the sea, to you
Meant for the time and the voice who pleads for all

You lay down guns spears and seas by the door
At the place where you were robbed of salt, you begin to sing
With the sea the patient space and survival
For all a world and a vine where finally time will open
Space is heavy inside us, woman, the sea is strong

Africa Africa O most joyous o stanza o dense beauty
I dreamed, in you humanity intrigued its heavy exile
Now I have left depth for a visible face
Gypsum for iron and coral for fish
Here, my net is bare, here the African, woman, on the sand

And she takes the salt into her hair beautiful jay beautiful fruit
And perhaps finally we shall gather it, o perhaps.

Wounds

We go this digging; we know we last as long or weigh the same. At salt we cry out. It works on wounds. Is good for torture.

(I have seen the wise men who do not yield to beauty. They think they weigh their words but only pile up pot-bellied boredom.)

Beauty, in our sea's distance: we have to confess why your face is sweet, yet your hands hard, and your body now in knots, on the embers of our charcoal fires.

Beauty, beauty yet for unknown stars, beauty for peoples. And salt in seed, and rain for uncured lands.

I

This cry still on our lips for grain, for death.
The year grazed upon its ashes the shore
Left its sand on the wreckage of the sea.

O only with foam are we given the long, slow span.
Foam flies off. And as we fall silent
We see this cortege where beauty's flame
Was forsaken.
See the city pass and so many prows of fires. Cry out
That the cortege will heed us. Hail them. Silence, heavy
    passing.
(Flame, beauty, O woman, they have forgotten us.)

II

This wind hauled into your hair
Plies the instant bound its trade with fire
You play earth and water on your sands
Nightdweller who entered the lovely door
You are my night my earth my vow.

If I tell of you as dead not alive
Instantly you make your fires a sun
To torment the sleeping body where I lie.
Dead you are not damned either, the day's
Body is your beloved one.

III

They have passed, sea princes
They have purged us of the secret bay.
We count sands along with foam
The terror, the secret hope. Splendors
Of sparkling mirrors. Dark dark birds.

Horde! Sunset behind hills' descent! Sailing, bleeding ship.
So History passed. Far from this sand where we keep watch.
   An island
Hails us. We answer. Blood, naked lava-flows against the
   setting sun. Space
Where the house passes, birds—the stutterer calls you
But he will not enter the errant season.

Even had he seen, when the nights lit up, even had he seen
What could he have seen? The woman whom he sees not as
   woman but beauty
Had he seen the woman, even if, what would be his words,
   seeing beauty pass
The woman who is one, under escort, cloud and flame, pass by?
   Had he seen
The woman pass like a peaceful seal upon the year, far from the
   sand?

Even had he seen errant beauty pass?

IV

I am of the night but you in your adornment
Far from my cries into the night still remain
Errant, to see you the waves

Open me wide though nighttime yesterday they made a crowd
Of me with no joyfulness no presents a whole year.

One single bloody January eternally remains
To tarnish you itself
It is an edge ungilded a white scramble for spoils
O beauty howling as you mount the swells.

V

He saw the cortege of princes and courtiers pass. Swords
    flourished.
He saw the evening's sword flame in the evening's blood. Also
Victims who towed the solid boat, and on its prow fat bankers
Made an unminted star with flesh and fruit.

On the uppermost deck he saw their scales. Magi passed
Proclaiming the waters of the sea eternal
They filled the sea with a wake of words. On the shore
Adrift he saw time, splendors, bodies' nakedness.

This breath of beauty on its face. Disfigured
A woman blew on the red sails. Then
The wound's image, not the wound itself but its seal, was on
    his heart

And he saw inside it the woman unadorned.

VI

And have delivered you to fires not pure
You murmuring of my seas and you
Rare silence you came into me
I caught the silence in snares of an almeh

Lover so gentle so weary of going
Where brimmed the edge of this fierce mane
No sob is here to grab you, summer
Shrivels in fires that were your eyes.

VII

Not pure this cry. Clay where he put his breath. He says:
   Beauty
Of a world all at once capsizing, pass. The fire
Inside you shouts, it is the seas' vow.

But his song is not pure and his throat knots, inside him
He sees the woman then pass in the long cortege of setting
   suns.

Her hair rings out into the night—the hair is chains
Her hands bleed—they are the hands of peoples gone dry
Her body bears the weight of time, mixed with blood
She has the dreamy eyes of the forgotten dead
The movements of girls hauled into fire
Beauty beauty the world is there—it is your bruised body.

VIII

I named you beauty, consigning you this heavy shriek of wings
   in which you pass
Along with words heaped by steady torment on my fire, I have
   named you
Vertigo, you choose me in the clarity of your speech on the
   dying sea.

You took the wave in your fingers, lacing foam into the sky, wrecking
These words that beat against your sides. I named you
Beauty, woman, very gentle swell, path against the setting sun, you threw
Spray into the eye opened by this shore
Spray where I knew the long ago of death, the azure
Where I saw you—draped in wounds.

There I came to know the garment of wounds.

IX

Is there someone, O who is it, who sings and is wounded
Far away from us when the water moves aside
And am I in this sea and in the tide where
The errant woman wearied? Or in the self who opened impure spaces?

Or am I in this mirage of putrid brine
When our blood alone keeps its right mind
When leaden in the wound weeps the absence where she passes?

X

Asia he says, red-watered land where dying embers smoke.
Dead islands, arms outstretched, their hands palms burnt to cinder.
Hands with their fingerless palms knot a wash of ash into the sky.

A sun sprawled out so has drunk humble blood on the sea, so the man
Dreamt in that blind: with stars for quarry and men for bait.

XI

Lands. Roots gone silent. Africa and far from its name, islands
Abandoned in death agony, banished from the world, naked
With blood clogged by nights' burden
Polynesia dying dark he sights you
And denies you come with burden and means you be fruitless
The way we see a rooster in the gold of old corn die
A bitter glittering death.

Highest Noon

Then the sun, sole realm. Once the land of childhood, it still is so simply. All this wounded time finally coming down to the salt secret an island bears. Wanting to describe time is high ambition. All one can do is stretch the inner space where time's word reiterates, where its light murmurs.

I saw my island on its high wind. The salt of the poem finally laid down in the earth as it winds down.

I

Gentle lovely people, here is azure.

Lovely gentle toll, endlessly falling from your cry. Where is the rider of your night? The blaze on the mare's face as she assails the rock? This one, more mournful than night, swallowing all this blind wind, and imploring—it cries out to you.

Where is this unseen dust that slept between the stones? And the drowsy child on the mare. Stone known by hooves alone.

And tangling in your night there is no wind, sea, or mare whose face is blazed—
Save when dawn takes the rider by surprise.

II

The cliff has belayed its clay nest to the sea. The dock at last, long sung in the solemn city of his song. And sixteen times the wound on his hands' fan. At last the sound of chainlinks on the dock.

A word unshouted, for the arriving shipment. Now the anchor sets in a gulp of air. To land, the bay of prose not gloriously cried not songs of oars or jetties, but careening and trunks and papers.

The sky tightens its choke-knot (the dock a reef, no jolt or slowing) on the water-lapped home.

III

The men went in, sea roar bursting in their hearts.

And the best stood, the glare of splendid history in his eyes. Far within his eyes does he see the noblest of forests? And he cries out: I cry you. O encircled, o well-known.

He did not run, his mouth winnowing foam. Hear, he says, time is cracking. It is the woman in his eyes.

O does she lie there, more plain and naked than the smell of fried fish at sea?

Body's drum and finest bow, some men are coming. But the best has not spoken.

IV

There was this bird, one lone bird on our sand, and there was the woman in the song, and no one will say whether it was the woman or the forest falling in love, and there was this bitterness, one lone cloud, winnower of salt, like a sea vow unheard by the shore—and there was the cold cloud blooming from the stem, when it was time for sailing ships, forsaking wind, to return to a horizon of clays and oars.

There was this bird, black fixity against backwater creeks, that shiver.

V

This island, then these islands all-united, O name them.

Shout them forth. All I want in the sea is a fold of clays on the lookout. One whole foam laid low.

Where is the first? Where the woman stranger with a long-ago vow? An island, a wind? —And the sea lies. The vow dies. Like this rooster obligated by his corn.

You who endlessly slash and slaughter. Your clay has burned. Dead your hands. Shout the wind.

O sea, name these ghosts.

VI

Untie your soul. That a rider urging his animal into midday may name you. And give you another name day, far from the song.

And may he stop, rider. He inclines toward the moment, where the foam took its salt. He ties the beast to a barren lemon tree. And on a cook-fire sees the limpid flower, the greenest. He gazes on the crazed wood.

In the sky waves deeper than a charcoal blaze were flowing. The sea calls, when midnight is phosphorescent.

He does not remember the moment, when that bird touched down.

VII

As the word bursts upon the earth—and roots pull up where the wind already blows.

(No one go there, sleeper wonder-struck or keeping daylong watch, who cannot shake it off, with, all around, the long-ago bird. Where are you, exorbitant birds?)

Birds of the wind that will die, where are you? O so many wrecks. Then the song, the fervent hoe.

On one hand lightning things, sea winds, the flouted sea. But the poem making headway on the other.

(And if it still is a place the word does not know, it is right to acclaim it, this place. For the word knows its own sound at last. The nascent fire faints away on the nights' bow.)

What is this splendor? Building its landscapes from one rim of the word to the other?

And, where the shower raised its veil, these deserts that appeared?

Who is the one who walks between earthen words, begins endlessly the pace of the first syllable again?

It is over, it succumbs. It takes root in the air.

Among the roots, one with the vast wound, a man arose.

His place: the three-tiered foams, the muddy sword of beaches.

Anse Madame where the water lay; and Anse Noire, its unraveled rope stuffed into the rock.

And the July sea preyed on by black bulls.

O for the ones who slash and the ones who sing we shall have songs, as pure as the sword of black and caesarless victories.

And for the ones who slaughter blazes at midday, a dewless song of roses.

—I arise and I explore and I embrace the nameless country.

Acclamation

It was the salt in time's bowl. Nothing was left but an obscure urn of words. Is there a morning? The darkness of course bodes well—when words are shining on the steps up to the house. In this realm of our hands.

I

Fetch me mudflows sheets of metal mangos from the blaze
Let the limpid word go dry and barrenness be over
Where the straw was and every uncircled thing
It is time to halt vast errantry and it is time
To arm the song with continents
That hail us in passing in broad midday
O worry, salt left on death by foam, my black land
Take me into the summer that has no spring, O cry.

II

It is the town, silent in its clay. It is the green wood, shoring up the frame of night.

It is our own dogs, seen lapping between two winds. Strays. Hairless iron dogs, gaunt wizards of our absence, errant dogs. It is women, fierce cravings, and men, toothless mouths. Factories' roux, the year's vintages. I have not named the sea, married

To a black cry, separated from the black procession. O this land
Closes down the sea and against the sound of peoples coming
Pulls shut its sandy handles, with their rock bolts.

III

I made such a cry my home, where no earth looms; and no shore is by the seas where I have been.

Twisted by the hurricane, this man sees the mud at the door, the path leading to nights where each one gutters on the verge of death

And he hears the earth where more than one name was buried.

IV

Hear the lands, behind the islet.

Yokes
(*1979*)

Note: In *Caribbean Discourse,* trans. J. Michael Dash (Charlottesville: University Press of Virginia, 1989), Glissant describes *Yokes* (*Boises*): "The closed texts of *Boises* resemble the concise riddles played out in *Tim-tim boiseche*: '—A barrel with no bottom? / —Wedding ring!' They track down the void, through overly measured explosions. Through the aberration of assimilation our one and only season was closed in upon itself. Now the islands are opening up. The word requires space and a new rhythm. 'I see moving forward through the land the inspired people we shall be' " (238; trans. modified).

*to every country that turns away
and grows incensed at running dry*

Yesteryear

Gorée

He inhabited his cry treefull: his roots spilled into ravines shouting out.

He knotted into time's gorge rawness from the deeps, and stayed many a wind-bare sail with his gaze.

He had no room to call upon surpassing, once steered between coast and bluff shore, in the harbor island where yesterday's dreams garrotte dreams of tomorrow to their death.

Slash and Burn

>   yoke
>   shackle
>   ball-and-chain
>   drag (gag of peppers, studded ear)
>   four-post
>   stocks

>   we do not trace the scars of our stripes.

Note: Off the coast of Senegal the now enslaved Africans awaited the voyage to the Americas on the island of Gorée. (Trans.)

Fats

In a breath of green, panting breeze, see trickling eye-level salty boredom of white butter, plump princess, staying put this toiling woman bragging on paddle marks, a pennysworth of lard, and shriveling dry the humble red beaten pad of fat alongside: our empty openings.

We hasten into dry leaves and hard mud.

Note: This is a tableau of the pre–World War II plantation markets in Martinique, a culture now lost. The women displayed on banana leaves three grades of fat for sale: the most expensive, white butter; then the cheaper, lard; and the cheapest, red fat. (Trans.)

House for the Dead

Rosary-driven dry old women gaping. We, acolytes bister
   cassocks in Roman sandals who bathe in sunlight. The red-
   head priest
naked from dust, drowned in a dream of shade
or maybe by his toe returned to Canada
whence he came.

Note: Before burial the bodies of those who died in the surrounding countryside were brought to town, and the wake would be held in a building near the church that served only this purpose. The same old women were always present—sort of professional mourners—telling their rosaries. The local children served as acolytes to the white priest, here suffering from the heat and cramped toes as he kneels. (Trans.)

Behanzin

He burns, shrunken star from this deepest sun; in the mirror of our whitewash his wives scattered about him.

Not one oh wind knew him. Nor jeered him, to extol villainy in raucous laughter at his *kora*.

In our minds knowing all the ins and outs the king recrowned laughs our lunacy, cries our night, dies our denials.

Note: Behanzin was a king of Dahomey exiled with all his wives to Martinique from Africa, which in folk tradition is not "darkest Africa" but the land of the "deepest sun." The *kora* is an African instrument. (Trans.)

What Begins

Country

    The child does not separate intact from the sphere, not in any sort of globe engrossed in log-wood, the child
    Rolls on his breakage belly an orb snot running toward the black tumescence
    of his navel.

Iron-dogs

Grey strays
consuming with errantry day's ardor, weighted
with a block better than dread scorching dreams
they end up dropped in the canal
in countless clawed
agonies.

Note: The *chiens-fers,* "iron-dogs," are small, hairless dogs apparently indigenous to Martinique. Mostly strays now, they are periodically rounded up, using poison bait, and thrown into the water. (Trans.)

Our Letter Will Be Called

We shall not beg, hand to bar the way
Nobly clad law suits us gleaming curbed
Lined up for insect honor
Its elytron spelled out from sweat to blood.

Country

Sun
green measure born of a hollow
of sea's kidney
of drunkenness in the chicken coops we row

into the blue they quarter

Note: To "row one's chicken coop" is to struggle in wretched destitution. The chicken coops leave the world of folk metaphor to become solid: stacked alongside the docks, they are reflected in the sea and "quarter" it. (Trans.)

On the Square: Savane

He gives vent thick and fast arms urgent
Hails his shadow on rock
Slams some enemy on the rutted track sunlit
Nails him with whirlwinds (arms dead)
Thrashes him with broken words
Falters
Forevermore closed painless
eyeless lawless windless

Note: Savane is the name of the public square in Fort de France, a square frequented by men who in their "verbal delirium" personify the nonproductive language of internalized colonial domination. (Trans.)

Elited Prose

He filters golden speech through the quick of his mind, knows how sheep is threaded on a spit, could have taken charge in Africa (an aide to the colonies), chews alamanda mixed with suet, is not the Trojans but Hector whom they hunt, vacations in Real France, is nigger but universal, adapts his level as he goes along, in short has faith in Man.

Note: This, then, would be another nonproductive use of language, overattentive to being "cultivated," dropping a reference to Racine's example of the exceptional: Hector not the Trojans. (Trans.)

Still a Factory

Gnawed tortoise
of an oozing tree
it moves projected transparent
on the roadside read as
ghosts already, shopping-centered.

Country

A worn conch inebriates me
its red vein paled in the iris of its blue
I explore it fill it with sands of pain
(ours is sea calamity asleep ashore at noon)

into the silent ravage, with all my might
I blow.

From Elsewhere

To changeless cries each rends the other's arm
How many armless men this same machete carves
Since yesteryear on the *mornes* their hocks
Fume severed future.

Wood of the Heights

Prose

When rosetrees calve from dream alone, let us be;
so from shout sparking into star and ember too much written
we beat out language, long sunk in its ravine
like unspeech hobbling in the mangrove,

harder than briarwood more
unbearable than a yoke.

Dlan

You cry you roam your weight your loins conjoin you and the earth that you defend you drift you kick: how many bygone days flights of years have you enlaced it in the din where lies your bed; this is beast couched as early as time's footstep in sapwood of roots who cries
   (Dlan Dlan Dlan come down again)

Dlan

Anyone who burns his eyes with oven smoke has seen womb and shadow: the unknown swelled into leaf before him, dogs far behind sniffed out the trail, the stand of acacias pinned him to new-composted land (into piercing tossing vertigo and he cries)
   Dlan Dlan Dlan come down again

Dlan

The night of ropes up there ensnares you you cry you roam see the shudder the mass lighten when pierced into cries, naked black turned into dentate leaf, you drift, hardly dare set foot on burning overturned: just as in early times, amazed he saw his forest growing bright with heat and wind, maroon he came down utterly replete with age.

Note: Dlan is the name of a wandering character in *Malemort* (Paris: Seuil, 1975), a novel in which Glissant explores questions of individual and collective relations to the sacred.

The Naysayer

When the hilltop gives way sheer to the easiness of depths, there where shadow wears ferns wreckage wind, what is the trail of leaves, the old-time woodfoot* and stagnant reek alluring and ensnaring?

The Naysayer

Master of ropes of bamboo of shadow holes where the smell of midnight sours.

The earth dresses, begins to burn. But the embracing sea, is dried by rocks among caned leaves.

But the sea.

---

* A *pied de bois d'antan*—from the Creole *piéboi,* meaning "tree". (Trans.)

Trace

Of this instant the dream where we are crawling: from hairless dogs in a fracas of acacias and dust to those calm skilled others from elsewhere, sheepdogs with a taste for Vietnamese, wolves who rehash some bit of African

retired here to a lair deserved: just look, the pact we've made with dogs,

in this morning of distant war we pray that five and twenty years from now they will love us never never will they eat us will not eat us not.

Role

Deluding us that the play mounted through our willpower, that we name act and dénouement in the world: knowing if they will take shape and fall in future from the tangle of the final day comic or tragic; or instead would glue themselves to a curtain never raised, stuck to an indistinct earth, one liquified.

Ashes

carnival
of chants instead of hills and dominoes instead of ritual masks

helmets burst by straw where the moon nails you and lost
dried up things instead of living ones and organdy instead of sacks

down the dead streets of the city, in a night of death or pale afternoon.

Tongue

The star grinds out the letter, it's a townhall ballot box. Every no-vote comes out yes. Mr. Lesprit's* secret stock.
Oh! For a rock!

---

* M. Lesprit was a mayor in Martinique. (Trans.)

Country

In the southward trek of lands. In the salty frost of morning. In the energy of clay earthing over this fate. In hands their palms now obsolete. In the voice of infinity through deserts and torrents. In the echo with neither wave nor roar. In begging. In a wound deep into dark greens. In the mud uprooting bamboos from cement, and in a naked old man alert all night for lightning. In a dead body scooped up in the trucks. In crawling. In a crazed driver leaving his tractor pale. In preciosity. In the jaws of a political and lying fish. In the heart-pang of rocks your whole heart. Where every land has come to you.

Deafer than Sea

We sink down companions
shell upon shell into harsh and unlearned skin
Outside the living where we hurtle dropped earth
Not seeing our sap's upleap
No hand glued to the tuff
All against all forever in the hardly secret
Laughter of the sailor.

And I deafer than sea sent my wild shots into One's field
From a basket winnowing words beyond the clay knife
Sulfured with rocks that here cracked open
The other story.

Words of a sailor a visitor
a getaway stiff and dead from his world inside
and overwhelmed by his face so much so that you cheer
ah how nice
you all are.*

---

* The final words—"the moral of this story" of alienated history—are a metamorphosis of certain famous words pronounced by a visiting de Gaulle as he looked out upon the cheering citizens of Martinique: "Ah, qu'êtes-vous français!" (Ah, how French you all are!) (Trans.)

Malemort

Saltworks

When you try only to work or earth over perhaps, stroll stone after stone into the far South. You will see the sad foam veer off at Devil's Table Rock.

Country

Too late: the aconite carves a white wake through us
Dreams of sand hollow us out beyond lust
Grey dogs we cry out in a scant smile
Gaping deserts from ourselves.

Fine Men

You sing of humanity you the defeated who dropped
The leaf of absence faded in the forest your pollens
Lapsing long ago, you cannot see ahead
You bleat out humanity lose flesh in your wind
From your face oh flimsy crowd.

Ray of Green

Sands eaten away by livid
We watch and wait for startled spark
To lay us out at last worn-out, to pale
We are wasping time.

Vaval

with stalk and striation
without one blaze within one calyx
we burn down giants we wet their ash
poetry of clay worn thin

Mangrove Fruit

Fruitless that the mangrove provides for crabs
Its refuge now tatters of the dead in leaf
Plaster and rubble send refugees
Down the runway adjacent where it drones.

Note: Vaval is an enormous Carnival figure, usually a caricature of some current political figures or someone "in the news." It is set on fire near the sea on Ash Wednesday and burns until it falls into the water. Then everyone makes a great show of weeping to mourn the death of Vaval. (Trans.)

Note: Crabs frequently invade the airport runways in Lamentin, where construction has encroached on the mangrove swamps bordering a cemetery. (Trans.)

Poetics

Understanding time heat
Rock heat
wedded pain
cry vaporing its word
vowel to vowel
concreted.

Monomagic

Cactus

On the ridge jagged fangs to monsoon
They still time's pollen
They brighten the stroke of noon
Handled by none
They vanish into days bygone.

In Reality

When I see us marshal flattery to our faces, harvesting foam splashed upon the docks: two Bostonians, some joker from Salento, a shilly-shally, all clods

I sense these factories are naked zombies of the afternoon O! how we leaf ourselves out
    to be their imbecilants.*

---

* Glissant's neologism *drôlataires* is created on the model of *locataires,* meaning "tenants." The inhabitants of Martinique, so eager to receive tourists, only achieve a comic mockery of production. (Trans.)

Schedule of Instruction

In offering to an obvious Visitor, the fat around our teeth, and our obsequious hands, palm down.

Informed by him how sweet the flower finds the pistil, we are grateful.

Should the Arrival deign to mention us—after a drink—it will be our pleasure to graft our knowledge to his Zenith.

Arcs

He prowls the waters setting out the roots of sea glass. What vow bends the masts and defoliates the eye? He has sealed a decree of chasm between two worlds.

You never build in the bow of the rainbow.

Fiefs

Faith or not
How he coils at the word, where mastered, the flame

Faith or not as he says holds groaning, so little saying

Whatever Opens Up

Ideal

Universal oh universal we run dry Sahel we flower *derrisle**
What llamas bear us any message for our kiddos at Roche-
  Carrée
Water is thick for us with blinds with space from our homes
  our bodies
Have drunk the hevea of yesterday and tomorrow O we puddle
  Universal

Ash and Ball and Chain

The earth grows bright, forsaking us in fluid scraps. It flies from our chests, our hands. We flow faint in the din. An enemy uproots something somewhere, we gather, we shiver, we insult each other in unison. As for the ones not there, calmly curse them. The absent trample an army, beyond the *mornes*. What do you bet the earth will gush into our heads, thick.

Strike

When, dead tired from waiting out the iris in the morning
  they slip off
About to drop screaming as if bagged alone
Arms are where they hit: All the maroons who have no arms
Drive their hands to ax a shoulder for crime unknown.

---

* *Derrisle,* a neologism, combines the words *derrick* and *isle.* (Trans.)

"Within the Budding Pineapple Grove"

The promised bird of rescue winged them with its opal
They dropped into our voices like wounded blocks and tackles
    hoed
With a machete the flatfaced leaves plastered with blood.

Note: There are two literary references in the title: Proust's "À l'ombre des jeunes filles en fleur" (translated by Scott-Moncrieff as "Within a Budding Grove") and scenes from a novel by Pierre Benoit romanticizing life in the Antilles. Benoit describes lovers embracing in the shade of the pineapple trees. The pineapple plant rarely excedes three or four feet in height, and the shade of its thick, spiny leaves would be hard for a human of normal stature to enjoy.

As in the former poem, this is a tableau of a massacre following a strike by workers—this time on a pineapple plantation, where the "birds of rescue" are government helicopters. (Trans.)

Guadeloupe

Let us breathe sighs of contentment our neighbor has denied his bondage o let us lock up privilege in wicker baskets ports and *drosers* container ships O well have we chosen the dark jewel becomes us breathe sighs of contentment the neighbor will grow alone in meagre repletion where partygoers what is freedom to us?

These

In us—underside of sand—jolt proclaiming the soul's yes to any passerby.
But see—heart of rock—the knot of flame gorging us and building blaze of this cry.

Garrotte

We had no word not from you. Any relish for going degradation and sameness desiccated, making us this way.
We sail our words in the very depths of flattening exposure.

Tomorrows

No hinterland at all. You, unable to withdraw behind your face
Reasons to unfold this running dry to plunge into all the absence, till through twisting detours you revive, black in the rock.